A Guide for Using

The Whipping Boy

in the Classroom

Based on the novel written by Sid Fleischman

This guide written by Jayne Merriman Yount

Teacher Created Resources
6421 Industry Way
Westminster, CA 92683
www.teachercreated.com

ISBN: 978-1-55734-920-0

©*1997 Teacher Created Resources*
Reprinted, 2013
Made in U.S.A.

Edited by
Ellen Woodward

Illustrated by
Howard Chaney

Cover Art by
Sue Fullam

Table of Contents

Introduction

A good book can touch our lives like a good friend. Within its pages are words and characters that can inspire us to achieve our highest ideals. We can turn to it for companionship, recreation, comfort, and guidance. It also gives us a cherished story to hold in our hearts forever.

In *Literature Units*, great care has been taken to select books that are sure to become good friends!

Teachers who use this literature unit will find the following features to supplement their own valuable ideas.

- Sample Lesson Plans

- Pre-reading Activities

- A Biographical Sketch and Picture of the Author

- A Book Summary

- Vocabulary Lists and Suggested Vocabulary Activities

- Chapters grouped for study, with each section including:

    - quizzes

    - hands-on projects

    - cooperative learning activities

    - cross-curriculum connections

    - extensions into the reader's own life

- Post-reading Activities

- Book Report Ideas

- Research Ideas

- A Culminating Activity

- Three Different Options for Unit Tests

- Bibliography

- Answer Key

We are confident that this unit will be a valuable addition to your planning and hope that as you use our ideas, your students will increase the circle of "friends" they can have in books!

Sample Lesson Plan

Each of the lessons suggested below can take from one to several days to complete.

Lesson 1

- Introduce and complete some or all of the pre-reading activities found on page 5.
- Read "About the Author" with your students. (page 6)
- Read the book summary with your students. (page 7)
- Introduce the vocabulary list for Section 1. (page 8)

Lesson 2

- Read chapters 1–4. As you read, place the vocabulary words in the context of the story and discuss their meanings.
- Select a vocabulary activity. (page 9)
- Learn about the Newbery medal and design a book medal for a special book. (page 11)
- Learn about castles and draw a dream castle with a partner. (page 12)
- Write a haiku. (page 13)
- Make a list of items necessary for survival in the wilderness. (page 14)
- Administer Section I quiz. (page 10)
- Introduce the vocabulary list for Section II. (page 8)

Lesson 3

- Read chapters 5–8. As you read, place the vocabulary words in the context of the story and discuss their meanings.
- Select a vocabulary activity. (page 9)
- Make a crown fit for a prince or princess. (page 16)
- With a partner, identify and write similes. (page 17)
- Write a character sketch for one of the characters in *The Whipping Boy*. (page 18)
- Identify the benefits that come with reading and writing. (page 19)
- Administer the Section II quiz. (page 15)
- Introduce the vocabulary list for Section III. (page 8)

Lesson 4

- Read chapters 9–12. Place the vocabulary words in the context of the story and discuss their meanings.
- Select a vocabulary activity. (page 9)
- Write a ransom note. (page 21)
- Create a recipe using the ingredient garlic. (page 22)

- Complete an information cube on rodents. (page 23)
- Recall the experience of being a role model. (page 24)
- Administer the Section III quiz. (page 20)
- Introduce the vocabulary list for Section IV. (page 8)

Lesson 5

- Read chapters 13–16. Place the vocabulary words in context and discuss their meanings.
- Select a vocabulary activity. (page 9)
- Make an origami book. (page 26)
- Make a compass. (page 27)
- Study cardinal directions and draw a compass rose. (page 28)
- Begin "Friendship Journal." (page 29)
- Administer Section IV quiz. (page 25)
- Introduce the vocabulary list for Section V. (page 8)

Lesson 6

- Read chapters 17–20. Place the vocabulary words in context and discuss their meanings.
- Select a vocabulary activity. (page 9)
- Make a board game. (page 31)
- With a group, write a newspaper article. (page 32)
- Invent a problem-solving device to catch rats. (page 33)
- Discuss fears and ways to overcome them. (page 34)
- Administer Section V quiz. (page 30)

Lesson 7

- Discuss any questions your students may have about the story. (page 35)
- Assign book report and research projects. (pages 36 and 37)
- Begin work on a culminating activity. (pages 38–41)

Lesson 8

- Administer Unit Tests: 1, 2, and/or 3. (pages 42–44)
- Discuss the test answers and possibilities.
- Discuss the students' enjoyment of the book.
- Provide a list of related reading for your students. (page 45)

Before the Book

Before beginning *The Whipping Boy*, help stimulate student interest and enthusiasm by completing the following activities and discussing the following questions:

1. Look over the book cover. What do you think a whipping boy is? What do you think the story might be about?

2. Have you read any other books by Sid Fleischman? What were they like? (Have several other books by Fleischman on hand to share and compare. See the list on page 45.) Who is the illustrator of this book? What is the copyright date?

3. What does the gold seal on the cover mean? Have you read any other Newbery Medal books? Name them. (Have other Newbery Award winning books on hand to share with the class.)

4. Have you ever visited a castle? If so, what was it like? If not, what do you think it would be like?

5. Have you ever run away from home? What were some of the problems you encountered?

6. Have you ever been punished for something you did not do? How did you feel inside?

7. What is your definition of a *brat*? What is the dictionary definition of a brat? How do most people feel about brats?

8. Have you ever seen a rat? How do most people feel about rats? Is there anything good about rats?

9. Have you ever been underground? How did you feel about that?

10. Can you name any living princes? If so, do you think they have whipping boys? Why or why not?

11. Brainstorm a list of words relating to:

   • royalty

   • poverty

   • survival

   • friendship

About the Author

Sid Fleischman was born on March 16, 1920, in Brooklyn, New York. He was the son of Reuben and Sadie Fleischman. He grew up in San Diego, California. As a boy, Sid Fleischman was influenced by his father, who loved to tell stories.

After he graduated from high school, Fleischman traveled with a vaudeville act, performing magic tricks. His love of magic is evident in his writing, as his stories are full of anticipation and fun. Fleischman keeps his readers guessing as to what may happen next.

During World War II, Sid Fleischman served in the Philippines, China, and Borneo in the United States Naval Reserve. He married Betty Taylor in 1942. They have three children: Jane, Paul, and Anne. Paul is also an author of children's books, just like his father.

Fleischman graduated from San Diego State College in 1955 with a B.A. degree. He then became a reporter for the *San Diego Daily Journal*. He also worked as a script writer for the television show *3-2-1 Contact*.

Fleischman has won many awards for his work, including the Lewis Carroll Award in 1969 for *McBroom Tells the Truth*. For *The Ghost on Saturday Night*, he won the Young Hoosier Award from the Association for Indiana Media Educators. For his book *Humbug Mountain*, he won the Boston Globe-Horn Book Award for Fiction and was a National Book Award finalist as well.

Sid Fleischman has also won the prestigious Newbery Medal from the American Library Association in 1987 for *The Whipping Boy*. Of this award, he said, "I stumbled across the catapulting idea for *The Whipping Boy* while researching historical materials for another project. I checked the dictionary. "A boy," it confirmed, "educated with a prince and punished in his stead." Fleischman originally intended to write the story as a picture book. He struggled with this approach. Once he decided to write *The Whipping Boy* in the form of a novel, the ideas flowed freely.

About winning the Newbery Medal, Fleischman said, "It's bliss. It should happen to everyone." *

*Something About the Author, Vol. 59

The Whipping Boy

by Sid Fleischman

(Available in USA, Troll, 1987; Canada, Vanwell Publishing; UK and AUS, Penguin)

The spoiled, incorrigible, young Prince Horace is better known far and wide as Prince Brat. Fortunately for Prince Brat, spanking the heir to the throne was unthinkable. Unfortunately for an orphan named Jemmy, he must serve as the royal whipping boy.

When the bored prince decides to run away, he orders Jemmy to accompany him as a manservant. Thus, the two boys begin a fantastic adventure that ultimately changes their lives.

Soon after their departure from the kingdom, the runaway boys are kidnapped for ransom by two bumbling crooks named Cutwater and Hold-Your-Nose Billy. Although Prince Brat and Jemmy escape their captors, the two highwaymen give chase throughout most of the story.

Prince Brat and Jemmy encounter a dancing bear named Petunia, and they are befriended by Petunia's owner, Betsy, and Captain Harry Nips, the Hot-Potato Man.

With Cutwater and Hold-Your-Nose Billy still in hot pursuit, Jemmy and Prince Brat enter the underground sewer system where Jemmy spent much time with his rat-catcher father while still living on the streets. Here our boys encounter darkness, rats, and Ol' Johnny Tosher before their hair-raising adventure comes to a close.

Throughout their ordeal, the Prince begins to see himself as others see him. He comes to admire and respect Jemmy's many strengths. He strives to be more like Jemmy. Prince Brat also learns to appreciate the common man. Jemmy, in turn, becomes more tolerant of the prince. By the end of their journey, Jemmy and Prince Brat have established a true and binding friendship.

Vocabulary Lists

On this page are vocabulary lists that correspond to each sectional grouping of chapters. Vocabulary ideas can be found on page 9 of this book.

Section I (Chapters 1–4)

furious	ferret	wicker	sewer
defiantly	reckon	protested	insolent
contrite	smirk	dreadful	hollow
exasperation	contrary	astonishment	maze
gloat	rascal	gallows	

Section II (Chapters 5–8)

garlic	thatched _roofed_	scheme _plan_	scoundrel
ruffian	hospitality	quill _spine_	generously _abundantly_
heir	herring	arrogant	paltry _sm. amount_
rogue _rascal_	bleat _sound of goat_	airs	ransom _rescue_
crest	vagabond _wanderer_	sacred _holy_	
villain	veal		

Section III (Chapters 9–12)

plague	outlaw	genuine	vanish
ration _measure_	indifference _unconcerned_	dumb	burrowing
contemplated - _thought_	treason _disloyal_	vile	truss _brace, beam_
regal - _royal, kingly_	decisive _determined_	imposter	hesitation
obedient	pretense	pitchpipe - _baton stick_	cutthroats _killer cruel_

Section IV (Chapters 13–16)

thoroughbred	coiled	ventured	ante
glimpse	amber	embankment	plunder
betrayed	barnacle	mired	satisfaction
foliage	grimy	enamel	

Section V Chapters (17–20)

greyhound	fowl	derelict	dumbfounded
rein	fathom	barge	befuddled
winced	ignorance	fret	noose
hazards	gnarled	haughtiness	bellow
immense	balked	manacle	notorious
turf	decree	elation	

8

Vocabulary Activity Ideas

You may choose to do these activities with the entire class or divide students into small groups and have each group select a different activity.

1. **Dictionary Races** — Distribute dictionaries to students. Write a vocabulary word on the board or overhead projector. When you say "Go!" students race to be the first to locate the word in the dictionary. The winner of each race reads the definition, part of speech, and gives a sentence using the word. You may write this information on the chalkboard or overhead projector for the class to copy. This activity reinforces dictionary skills and vocabulary, as well as providing a study sheet for students. Remind students to use guide words.

2. **Jeopardy** — Make flashcards for vocabulary words, writing the word on one side and the definition on the other. Laminate the cards and tape them to the wall or chalkboard, definition side out. Students form two teams. Players take turns selecting a card. After reading the definition aloud, the player must give the correct vocabulary word in order to earn a point. The team with the most points wins.

3. **Telephone** — This activity is more fun for children if you have two discarded telephones available for their use. Otherwise they can pretend to use the telephone. Divide students into pairs. Each pair must write a telephone conversation using at least 10 vocabulary words throughout the conversation. The pairs then share their conversation in front of the class, one pretending to call the other and then reciting the dialogue they have prepared.

4. **Word Search** — On graph paper, have students make word search puzzles, using vocabulary words. Students may trade puzzles with each other and try to find as many words as they can.

5. **Vocabulary Pairs** — Have students choose 10 pairs of words from their vocabulary list that can be linked together in a sentence. Using each pair of words, instruct students to write meaningful sentences related to the story. An example might be: "The *ruffian* named Hold-Your-Nose-Billy loved *garlic*."

6. **Vocabulary Ball** — Before a quiz or for a quick review, toss a lightweight ball to a student. Give the student a definition and ask him/her to name that word. After answering, the student tosses the ball back, and the process is repeated with another student.

7. **Writing Adventure** — Have students write a one-paragraph adventure of the legendary King Arthur and his knights, using at least five vocabulary words.

8. **Synonyms/Antonyms** —- Review the meanings of synonyms and antonyms. Working in small groups, have students look over the last section of their vocabulary words. Ask them to find as many synonyms for the word *ruffian* as they can. Choices might include words such as *rogue*, *scoundrel*, *rascal*, *highwayman*, *villain*, *outlaw*, and *cutthroat*. Then, ask students to brainstorm a list of antonyms for words such as *hero*, *role model*, *knight-in-shining-armor*, *gentleman*, etc. Ask them to find other synonyms and antonyms within the list.

Quiz Time!

1. On the back of this paper, write a one-paragraph summary of the major events in each chapter of this section. Then, complete the rest of the questions on this page.

2. Describe Prince Brat. _____

   _____

3. Name one practical joke the prince plays on others at the castle. _____

   _____

4. What is the purpose of having a whipping boy at the castle? _____

   _____

5. How does Jemmy react to the whipping he receives? _____

   _____

6. Who is Master Peckwit? _____

   _____

7. How does Prince Brat feel about reading and writing? _____

   _____

8. What does Jemmy dream of doing upon his escape? _____

   _____

9. What is Prince Brat afraid of? _____

   _____

10. What happens to Prince Brat and Jemmy after they become lost in the fog? _____

   _____

   _____

Newbery and Caldecott Medals

Sid Fleischman received the Newbery Medal in 1987 for *The Whipping Boy*. Each year the Newbery Medal is given to the book that is judged to be the most distinguished contribution to children's literature in America. The award was established by Frederick Melcher in 1921. Mr. Melcher was the chairman of the board of a publishing company named R. R. Bowker Co. Mr. Melcher named the award for John Newbery, a printer and seller of children's books in England. John Newbery lived from 1713 to 1767. He is special because he was the first person to print and sell books for children. John Newbery was called the "friend of children."

Frederick Melcher also founded the Caldecott Medal. The Caldecott Medal is given to an illustrator each year for an outstanding children's picture book. Look up the Caldecott Medal in the encyclopedia to find out who it was named for, what it looks like, and to discover if you have read any Caldecott Medal books.

In the space provided, answer the following questions and then design a book medal of your own.

- For whom would you name your medal? _____

  _____

- Why is this person special? _____

  _____

- What is significant about the emblem or picture on your medal? _____

  _____

- What qualities would you look for in a book deserving of your medal? _____

  _____

Book Medal

Castle Sweet Castle

Castles have long been the settings for many children's stories, fairy tales, and nursery rhymes. Although Sid Fleischman gives us few details of Prince Brat's castle, we know enough about castles from other stories to form a picture in our minds. Brainstorm for a few moments with the students, asking them to name as many stories, fairy tales, nursery rhymes, and poems involving castles and kings as they can. Here are a few examples:

Snow White and the Seven Dwarfs

Cinderella

Rapunzel

Rumpelstiltskin

Sleeping Beauty

Dick Whittington and His Cat

The Emperor's New Clothes

"Old King Cole"

"Humpty Dumpty"

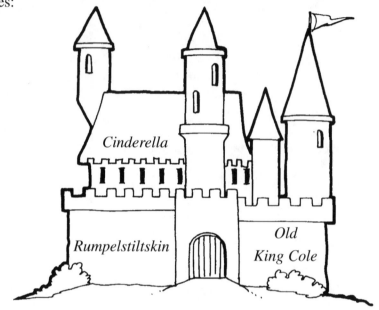

Provide students with several resources so that they can research castles or share the following information with them:

Castles were homes and fortresses of kings and noblemen, beginning around A.D. 900. As well as providing a home, a castle helped the king defend the land on which it stood.

Although early castles were made of wood, they were later constructed mostly of stone. Walls could be up to 33 feet (10 m) thick. This provided great protection from enemies and fire. Most castles were built on hillsides or mountaintops and had round towers with cutouts called *crenels* through which arrows could be shot.

Deep ditches called *moats* often surrounded the castle to keep an enemy from reaching the castle walls. A drawbridge to the entrance across the moat could be raised if enemies approached.

Inside the castle, candles and torches were used for light, and fire was used for heat. Usually castles were damp and drafty. In addition to housing the king or nobleman's family, servants, priests, soldiers, and farm animals also resided there.

Have the students work with a partner to draw a picture of their dream castle and write a descriptive paragraph explaining the features offered in their dream castle. Encourage them to be creative!

Poetry Time—Haiku

Haiku is a popular form of Japanese verse. It is usually written in 17 syllables that are organized in three lines of five, seven, and five syllables. It does not rhyme, and it usually describes a special or beautiful moment in nature. It uses descriptive phrases to create a mood of wonder, phrases such as *indigo blue sky, scarlet ladybug, a tiny sparrow's chirping,* or a *soft velvet fog.* Here are two examples of haiku:

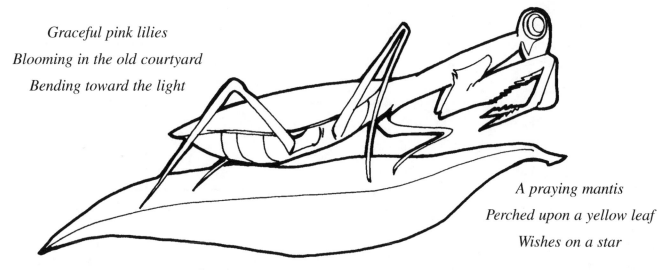

Graceful pink lilies

Blooming in the old courtyard

Bending toward the light

A praying mantis

Perched upon a yellow leaf

Wishes on a star

On page 9 of *The Whipping Boy*, Sid Fleischman describes the fog in which the runaway boys are lost:

"A thick fog had swirled in, they'd strayed from the road, and trees had closed in on them."

On page 15, Fleischman again described the fog, using these words:

"Wisps of fog clung like tattered rags to the trees, and then the forest cleared."

Recall a special time you have experienced while in the great outdoors. Perhaps you watched a baby animal at play, a rainbow, a shooting star, a tiny insect, or a misty morning. Write about your experience in haiku in the space provided below. Be sure to count the syllables in each line.

Name the topic._____ (five syllables)

Describe where it is. _____ (seven syllables)

Describe what is happening._____ (five syllables)

Now write a second haiku about fog._____

_____

_____

Survival

Before running away, Prince Brat had packed a basket of meat pies, fruit tarts, and roast pheasant. The moonlight served as their lantern in the night. Were these adequate provisions for surviving several days alone in the forest?

If you knew that you were going to be spending many days alone in a dense forest, what would you pack in your survival kit? Work with a partner and decide upon ten items that you would pack in your backpack. Remember, you are limited to items you can carry. Keep in mind the necessities of food, clothing, and shelter.

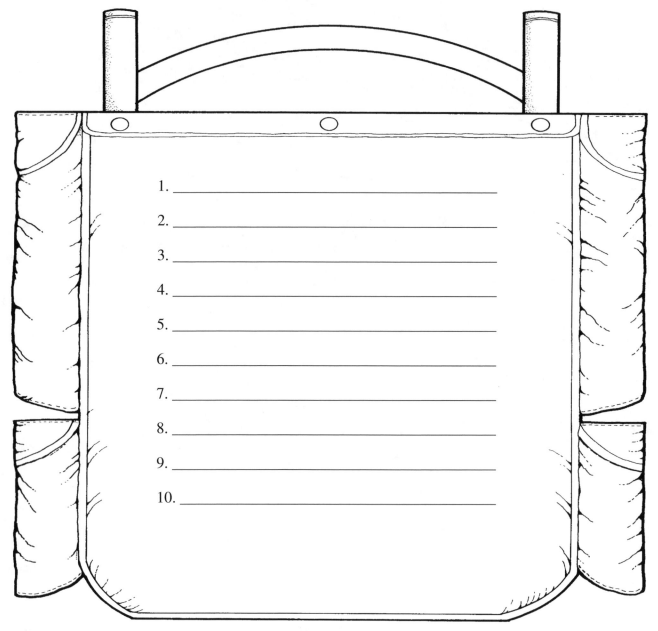

1. _____
2. _____
3. _____
4. _____
5. _____
6. _____
7. _____
8. _____
9. _____
10. _____

Brainstorm Activity: If you could take one book along, what would it be?

Quiz Time!

1. On the back of this paper, write a one-paragraph summary of the major events that happen in each of the chapters in this section. Then, complete the rest of the questions on this page.

2. Explain why Billy is called "Hold-Your-Nose Billy." _____

_____

3. Explain how Cutwater first becomes aware of the fact that Prince Brat and Jemmy are not ordinary boys. _____

_____

4. In what way has Jemmy previously heard of the highwayman, Billy?_____

_____

5. What is Prince Brat's real first name?_____

_____

6. Why does Jemmy think the prince is empty headed? _____

_____

7. Name three items that Prince Brat brings along in his wicker basket. _____

_____

8. Why do the outlaws believe that Jemmy is the true prince?_____

_____

9. What does Hold-Your-Nose Billy give Jemmy to use as pen and ink? _____

_____

10. What ransom do the bandits finally decide to ask for in exchange for the prince?

_____

_____

Crowning Glory

Digging around deeper in the basket, the garlicky outlaw called out to Cutwater. "Bring the lantern closer! What's this?"

In the gloom of the hut, the big man lifted out a golden crown. "That's mine!" bleated the prince. "Was yours," corrected Hold-Your-Nose Billy, placing the crown on the tangled red nest of his hair.

Every monarch must have a crown. Prince Brat evidently valued his crown, as he chose it as one of the few items he would take when he ran away. What do you think Prince Brat's crown looked like?

Design your own crown to fit your personality. Here are some suggestions to help you get started but use your imagination to personalize your crown.

Materials:

- 1 lightweight poster board strip 1" x 2' (2.5 cm x 61 cm)long
- construction paper
- stickers
- feathers
- glitter
- ribbon

- crayons
- markers
- glue
- Scotch tape
- straws
- any other desired materials

Directions:

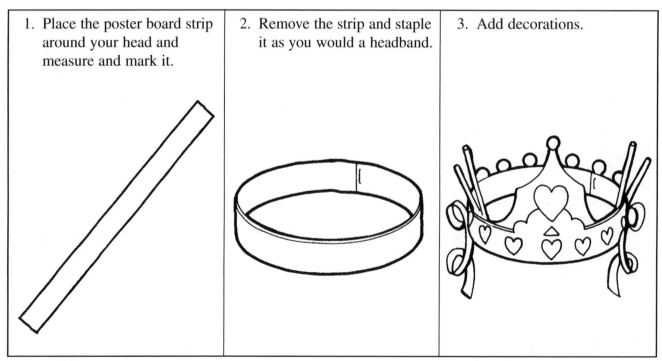

| 1. Place the poster board strip around your head and measure and mark it. | 2. Remove the strip and staple it as you would a headband. | 3. Add decorations. |

For a sturdier crown, add a second poster board strip to go over the top of the head.

16

Similes Galore

A simile is the comparison of two unlike things using the words *like* or *as*. *The Whipping Boy* is filled with rich comparisons of this nature. Here are a few examples:

Page 6 . . . "your tongue hangs out like a red flag!"

Page 7 . . . "the moon gazed down like an evil eye . . . ."

Page 21 "Prince Brat's face turned red as hot iron."

What two things do you think are being compared in each of these three sentences?

Skim through the first two sections of the book to locate other similes. Write them down on the lines below.

1. _____

2. _____

3. _____

4. _____

Here are some other familiar examples of similes:

- **mad as a hornet**

- **cool as a cucumber**

- **happy as a lark**

- **growing like a weed**

Work with a partner to create similes of your own. Then choose your best simile and illustrate it. Your illustrated pages can be bound together to make a class book of similes.

> Be on the lookout for similes as you continue reading *The Whipping Boy*. Think about how this type of writing adds color and humor to the story and helps the reader form a more vivid mental picture of the situation.

Character Sketch

Abraham Lincoln was a tall, lanky man with disheveled hair and penetrating eyes. He was honest, kind, and humble. Lincoln was a great man with a great vision.

Discuss physical traits and character traits with your students. Brainstorm a list of physical traits and character traits. Have two students record these responses on the chalkboard. Then ask students to write a character sketch about one of the characters in *The Whipping Boy*. The character sketch should be a paragraph in length and should include eight to ten character traits and physical traits.

When brainstorming, you may want to help students get started by suggesting some of the traits listed below:

Physical Traits		
• bald	• glamorous	• short
• bearded	• graceful	• skinny
• beautiful	• gray haired	• small
• blond	• handsome	• tall
• brunette	• healthy	• tan
• clean	• heavy	• ugly
• clumsy	• muscle-bound	• wrinkled
• freckled	• pretty	• young

Character Traits		
• angry	• gentle	• pleasant
• artistic	• happy	• regal
• brave	• honest	• sad
• clever	• imaginative	• shy
• cowardly	• intelligent	• sinister
• courteous	• jealous	• talented
• creative	• kind	• thoughtful
• dishonest	• optimistic	• wise

Just for Fun . . .

Just for fun, have the students create a character sketch of a pet, real or imaginary.

Reading and Writing

In chapter two of *The Whipping Boy*, we discover that Prince Brat can neither read nor write. "You fiddle-faddled scholar!" exclaimed Master Peckwit. "One day you'll be king! And you still don't know the alphabet from pig tracks!" In chapter seven we learn that Cutwater and Hold-Your-Nose Billy cannot read or write either. Therefore, Jemmy must write the ransom note for the villains.

Reading and writing enrich our lives in many ways. Most of us take our ability to read and write for granted, but without reading and writing our lives would be much more difficult. Make a list of all the ways you use reading and writing in your daily life.

Things I Read	**Things I Write**
restaurant menus	pen pal letters

What activity would you miss the most if you could not read or write?_____

_____

Quiz Time!

1. On the back of this paper, write a one-paragraph summary of the major events that happen in each of the chapters of this section. Then, complete the rest of the questions on this page.

2. What do you think Prince Brat learns about the eating habits of those less fortunate than he?

   _____

   _____

3. How does Cutwater intend to find out if the ransom note is written as he has instructed?

   _____

   _____

4. What is Jemmy's plan for returning the prince safely to the castle and freeing himself?

   _____

   _____

5. What item is Jemmy planning on sending back to the palace, supposedly to convince the king that the villains are genuine? _____

   _____

6. Why do you think the prince refuses to leave when he has the opportunity?

   _____

   _____

7. Why will the king know that Prince Brat did not write the ransom note?

   _____

   _____

8. Where does Jemmy hide in order to escape the villains?

   _____

   _____

9. Why does Prince Brat reveal Jemmy's hiding place to Cutwater?

   _____

   _____

10. Why does Jemmy suggest sending the king's horse back to the castle as a messenger?

   _____

   _____

A Ransom Note

To review the four parts of a letter, write an example on the board of each of these parts, using different-colored chalk to highlight each one.

Have the children write their own ransom letters to the king. Encourage students to be creative in making up the greeting, date, and ransom request.

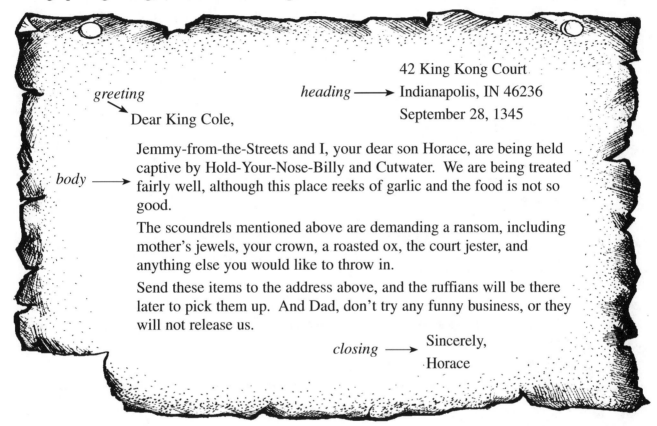

greeting

heading ⟶ 42 King Kong Court
Indianapolis, IN 46236
September 28, 1345

Dear King Cole,

body ⟶ Jemmy-from-the-Streets and I, your dear son Horace, are being held captive by Hold-Your-Nose-Billy and Cutwater. We are being treated fairly well, although this place reeks of garlic and the food is not so good.

The scoundrels mentioned above are demanding a ransom, including mother's jewels, your crown, a roasted ox, the court jester, and anything else you would like to throw in.

Send these items to the address above, and the ruffians will be there later to pick them up. And Dad, don't try any funny business, or they will not release us.

closing ⟶ Sincerely,
Horace

Now write your own ransom note.

A Pinch of Garlic

Hold-Your-Nose Billy was known for his affection for garlic. Garlic is a plant that is grown for its bulb, which is used to season or flavor foods. It possesses the same strong-tasting compound as the onion but in different quantities. The garlic bulb is made up of several small cloves. The cloves may be eaten, ground into powder, or squeezed for their juice.

With a partner, look through a cookbook and find a recipe calling for garlic as one of the ingredients. Examples would be garlic bread, garlic sticks, and spaghetti sauce or salad dressing. Copy the recipe down on the card below.

Recipe_____

From the kitchen of_____

_____

_____

_____

_____   Serves_____

Now create your own recipe using garlic. Make sure to create an especially delicious dish that Hold-Your-Nose Billy would like.

Recipe_____

From the kitchen of_____

_____

_____

_____

_____   Serves_____

You and your partner may wish to prepare one of these garlic recipes at home or in school.

For a popcorn treat, try peeling a clove of garlic and putting it in an air popper with the popcorn kernels. Remove the clove before serving. For microwave popcorn, try adding a little garlic salt to the prepared popcorn.

Teacher Note: Be sure to check with your students for food allergies before assigning this project.

Oh Rats!

While living in the castle as a whipping boy, Jemmy dreams of freedom and of going back to the sewers to catch rats for a living. Rats could be sold and used as fighters in dog-and-rat pits.

Today, rats might be used in scientific research or even as family pets. In the Middle Ages (1300's) rats caused a terrible outbreak of bubonic plague (also called Black Death) in Europe. The disease can be transmitted to a person from the bites of fleas from infected rats. Today, sanitation and rat control help to curb the spread of this disease.

How much do you know about rats and other rodents? Choose a rodent from the list below to research. The information you obtain will be used to make an Information Cube.

Rodents

rat	chinchilla	guinea pig	springhare
mouse	woodchuck	lemming	muskrat
gerbil	beaver	mole	hamster
capybara	squirrel	marmot	vole
jerboas	flying squirrel	prairie dog	dormouse
porcupine	chipmunk	kangaroo rat	agouti

Materials:

- pencil
- paper
- research materials
- small square tissue box
- glue
- white construction paper

Fold a piece of notebook paper into thirds. Place one of the following topics at the top of each square on the notebook paper, using front and back sides. As you research your chosen species, write key words or phrases in the appropriate square.

Topics:

- Physical characteristics (size, coloring)
- Habitat (country, land forms)
- Food (what it eats, how it gets food)
- Life cycle (how it develops from baby to adult, life span)
- Enemies
- Unique features (how it has adapted to the environment)

Directions

1. Measure and cut out construction paper squares to fit the top, bottom, and sides of the tissue box.

2. On each side of the box, write a few facts from each square of your note page.

3. Illustrate each square.

4. Glue the squares to the tissue box.

5. Share your information cube with the class.

These cubes may be hung from the ceiling or put on display in your classroom or school library.

Being a Role Model

Jemmy was a role model for Prince Brat in many ways. Prince Brat looked up to Jemmy and admired his courage.

Look at the chart below. Describe a situation in which Jemmy exhibits the admirable traits listed. Then describe a situation in your life when you exhibited some of the same characteristics and were a role model for someone else.

Character Traits	Jemmy	My Life
Bravery		
Dependability		
Generosity		
Honesty		
Kindness		
Responsibility		
Understanding		
Other		

Quiz Time!

1. On the back of this paper, write a one-paragraph summary of the major events that happen in each of the chapters of this section. Then, complete the rest of the questions on this page.

2. What wild beast does Jemmy meet in the woods as he makes his escape? _____

_____

3. How does Jemmy react when the prince forgives him for attempting to escape by himself?

_____

_____

4. Describe the relationship between Jemmy and Prince Brat in one well-written sentence.

_____

_____

5. When the boys meet Betsy in the woods, what is she looking for? _____

_____

6. Define "mudlarking." _____

_____

7. Who is Captain Harry Nips? _____

_____

8. Why does Jemmy ask the captain to go back for his friend? _____

_____

9. When the villains discover Prince Brat hiding inside the coach, does the prince betray Jemmy a second time? Explain your answer. _____

_____

10. When the villains whip Prince Brat, thinking he is the whipping boy, how does the prince react to the whipping?_____

_____

Tiny Origami Book

Discuss the following story elements with the students:

- characters
- setting
- problem
- rising action

- climax
- falling action
- solution

Have students identify these story elements in *The Whipping Boy* and other stories or fairy tales they have read. Once they have a good understanding of these concepts, have them write and illustrate an origami book of story elements from *The Whipping Boy*. The book should have eight pages. Have students design a book cover for page one and, on the other seven pages, write about the story elements. Illustrations should be included on each page.

Directions:

1. Fold a sheet of white paper into eight equal parts and then unfold it.	2. Fold it in half like this:	3. Cut the paper to the halfway fold as shown: 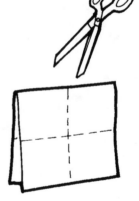
4. Open the paper up to show the cut.	5. Lengthwise, fold the paper in half and push the ends towards one another like an accordion.	6. Fold these ends together to make an eight page book.

Make a Compass

On page 48 of *The Whipping Boy,* Betsy tells Jemmy that the river is due south. She states that her Pa always said she had a head like a compass.

Making a compass is easy and fun. This activity can be done in cooperative groups if there are adult supervisors to ensure safety. Here are the materials your group will need:

- a pan of water
- a needle
- a flat piece of cork
- an alnico magnet

Directions

1. Rub the tip of the needle a few times on the south end of the magnet. This will magnetize the needle. (If using a smaller, weaker magnet, you may find it necessary to rub the needle across the south end of the magnet 30 or 40 times.)
2. Place the needle on the floating cork. The earth's magnetism will turn the needle around to point north.
3. After making the compass, locate south, east, and west.

To learn more about directions, each group should place their compass on or beside a map of the state in which they live. After locating their hometown or city, students should find the items listed on the chart below and, using the compass, should indicate whether these locations are north, south, east, or west of their hometown.

	Name	Direction
the state capital		
a state park		
largest river		
neighboring state		
neighboring state		
neighboring state		
large lake		
other		

A Rose Is a Rose

"Which way is south?" asked Jemmy. Betsy paused to set her arm like a signpost. "Straight on!" she said. Betsy knew her cardinal directions. The four directions—north, south, east, and west—are called cardinal directions.

On many maps and charts, you will find a small design called a *compass rose*. A compass rose is a direction finder that shows the cardinal directions. The compass rose is often ornamental in design. See if you can find one in your social studies book or on a classroom map.

Color the compass rose below and remember to add the cardinal directions!

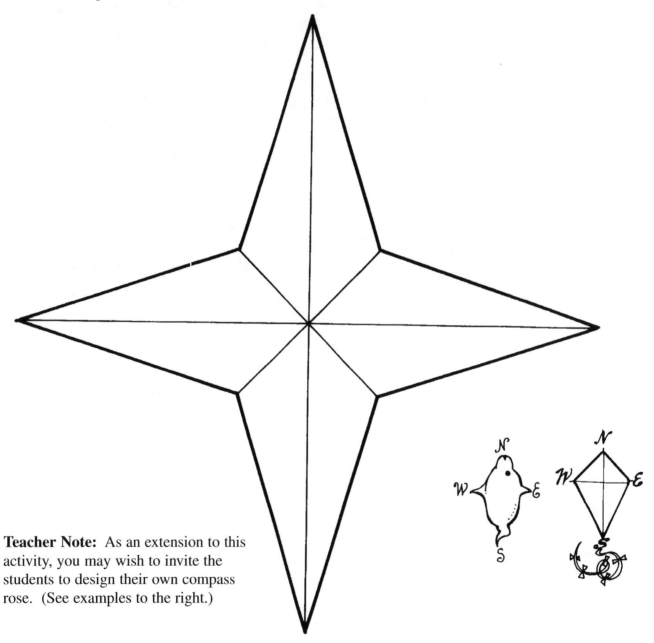

Teacher Note: As an extension to this activity, you may wish to invite the students to design their own compass rose. (See examples to the right.)

Encourage students to be imaginative. The sky is the limit! Papers may be bound into a class book or displayed on a bulletin board. If bound into a book, instruct students to leave a one-inch (2.5 cm) margin on the left-hand side of their papers for binding.

Friendship Journal

Jemmy and Prince Brat develop a true friendship over the course of their adventures, but, as you recall, they were not friends in the beginning. In chapter 6, Jemmy calls Prince Brat "empty-headed." In chapter 7, Prince Brat says Jemmy is a "witless servant boy." After spending time together and getting to know one another's strengths, however, they begin to develop admiration and even a fondness for each other.

Have the students make a friendship journal in order to get to know their classmates a little better. The journals can be made by folding five sheets of lined paper in half. Then have the students decorate a construction paper cover and staple the journals together. This will provide space for five entries and five responses. If you wish to use the journals for a two-week period, use 10 sheets of lined paper.

Give students 10 or 15 minutes each day to write about something they would like to share with their peers. Then have students trade journals for a response from a classmate. Instruct students to end their entries with a question. This will help the classmate who is responding to get started.

Announce that all journal entries must be of a positive nature.

Teacher Note: Grading suggestions for this activity can be found on page 47.

Quiz Time!

1. On the back of this paper, write a one-paragraph summary of the major events in each chapter of this section. Then, complete the rest of the questions on this page.

2. How does Jemmy feel about the prince being whipped by Hold-Your-Nose Billy?

   _____

   _____

3. What keeps the king's men from searching Captain Nips' coach after they stop it?

   _____

   _____

4. Why is Prince Brat momentarily confused when Smudge reaches out to shake the prince's hand?

   _____

   _____

5. How does the prince react when he learns that his subjects refer to him as "Prince Brat"?

   _____

   _____

6. According to the broadsides being peddled by a news seller, who is responsible for the prince's disappearance? _____

   _____

7. Who is Ol' Johnny Tosher? _____

   _____

8. Why is it dangerous to go under the brewery while down in the sewers?

   _____

   _____

9. How are Captain Nips and Betsy rewarded for their kindness to Prince Brat and Jemmy?

   _____

   _____

10. In one well-written sentence, describe the relationship between Jemmy and Prince Brat in chapter 20. _____

   _____

Fun and Games

The Whipping Boy is full of adventure and excitement from the point when Jemmy and Prince Brat are kidnapped by two highwaymen in the forest to the final chase through rat-infested sewers. Have students brainstorm a list of highlights from the book. Then divide students into cooperative groups in which they work to create a board game.

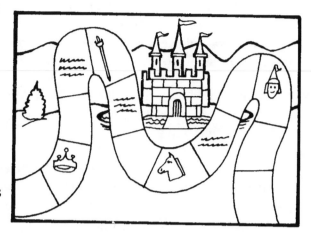

Instruct students to fill in the Brainstorm Work Sheet below and then draw their game on poster board. Each group should write a complete set of instructions to accompany their game.

Brainstorm Work Sheet

Game name _____

For _____ to _____ players

Ages _____ to _____

Objective _____

_____

Game pieces _____

Procedure_____

_____

_____

_____

Rules _____

_____

_____

Variation_____

_____

This activity may require two sessions to complete. Upon completion, have the groups trade their game boards with one another for a fun-filled afternoon. As an added treat, you might wish to provide a few snacks for the players such as Captain Nips' Potato Chips, Petunia's Popcorn, and Prince's Punch.

Extra, Extra, Read All About It!

Explain to students that in medieval times, kings often hired scribes to record special events. These written accounts were similar to our newspaper articles. On page 73 of *The Whipping Boy*, a news seller peddles *broadsides* proclaiming incorrectly that the prince had been sold to the gypsies. A broadside was an advertisement or story printed on one side of a sheet of paper.

Ask students what information should be contained in a news article. Should it be accurate? Why? Discuss the very important elements of *who*, *what*, *when*, *where*, *why*, and *how* in writing an accurate, informative account of an event.

Have students work in small groups to write the account of the kidnapping of Prince Horace and his whipping boy. Instruct the group recorders to make a list of important details. The group writer should then use these details to write a creative, informative, detailed account of the kidnapping. Have the group proofreader check for spelling and punctuation errors. The group reporter will then read the article to the rest of the class.

Following is a list of questions to help students get started.

Who, What, When, Where, Why, How

As a journalist for the *Knightly News*, it is your responsibility to write a front-page story of the prince's disappearance. In your notebook, record the following information to help write an accurate and informative article.

1. Who disappeared?

2. How did it happen?

3. Why did it happen?

4. What was the ransom request?

5. When did the incident occur?

6. Where did it happen?

Now arrange this information in paragraph form. Don't forget to include a big headline!

Problem Solving Inventions

On Jemmy's mudlarking expedition, he found an old birdcage with which to capture rats, but how do you suppose he lured the rats into the cage?

Working with a team of three or four classmates, think of five possible solutions to this dilemma. If you like, use a reference book to find out more about rats, such as foods they like to eat. How many rats do you think you might capture in one hour, using these methods? Make an estimate.

Possible Solutions
1. _____
2. _____
3. _____
4. _____
5. _____

Circle the number of the solution that you believe would be most effective. Choose a teammate to draw an illustration of it in the space provided below.

Afraid of the Dark?

Prince Brat was afraid of the dark and would not sleep without a lit candle. When he and Jemmy were hiding in the damp sewers, Prince Brat was terrified of the darkness and "had turned dead white." Are you afraid of something? Many people have fears. Some people are afraid of deep water. Some people are afraid of heights, while others are afraid of mice. Many people fear speaking or performing in front of an audience.

Sometimes just having a friend nearby helps us to face our fears and even overcome them. Jemmy said to the prince, "Don't fret about the dark! Hang on to me."

Draw a picture of your fear in the space provided. Then, with a partner, brainstorm a list of ways that might help you both overcome your fears.

My fear looks like this:

Possible ways to overcome my fear:

1. _____

2. _____

3. _____

Any Questions?

When you finished reading *The Whipping Boy*, did you have some questions that were left unanswered? Write some of your questions here.

_____

_____

_____

_____

Work in groups or by yourself to prepare possible answers for some or all of the questions you have asked above and those written below Give reasons for your answers. When you have finished your predictions, share your ideas with the class.

- Why should Prince Horace learn to read and write?

- Why would the king want to work at improving his relationship with his son?

- Do Betsy and Captain Nips come back to the castle to visit?

- Does Master Peckwit stay on at the castle as a tutor?

- Why isn't Prince Brat's mother, the queen, ever mentioned?

- What is the relationship between Jemmy and Prince Brat after their return to the castle?

- Is the true story of the prince's kidnapping ever printed in the broadsides?

- Do Betsy and Captain Nips lead different lifestyles after receiving their reward?

- Does Prince Brat ever tell the king about receiving a whipping from the villains?

- Would there be any reason to bring a new whipping boy to the castle?

- Why would Jemmy and Prince Brat want to see Smudge again?

- What becomes of Jemmy? Does he spend the rest of his life at the castle?

- How can Prince Brat and Jemmy become good friends when their backgrounds are so different?

- How could Prince Brat change the opinions of local peasants about himself?

- What becomes of Billy and Cutwater on the convict island?

- Does the strength and goodness Jemmy helped Prince Brat find in himself stay with him?

- Does Jemmy find a true home at the castle after all that has happened?

Book Report Ideas

There are numerous ways to do a book report. After you have finished reading *The Whipping Boy*, choose one method of reporting that interests you. It may be a way that your teacher suggests, an idea of your own, or one of the ways mentioned below.

- **See What I Read?**
  This report is a visual one. A model of a scene from the story can be created, or a likeness of one or more of the characters from the story can be drawn or sculpted.

- **Fairy Tale Fun**
  Retell the story of *The Whipping Boy*, incorporating a character from a fairy tale into the plot. You may have Prince Brat and Jemmy run into the Frog Prince or Rumpelstiltskin on their journey through the forest. You might also, for example, wish to use characters from *Rapunzel*, or *The Princess and the Pea*.

- **Parade Float**
  Using a shoe box, create a float that might be used in a parade celebrating the prince's safe return home. You may wish to have other characters ride on your float, such as Betsy and Petunia.

- **Be a Cartographer**
  Make a map of the forest within which Jemmy and Prince Brat become lost. Place additional sites on the map that are not mentioned in the book, such as roadside picnic rests, overnight lodging, waterfalls, caves, etc.

- **Commercial**
  With a partner, write a commercial for a real or imaginary food item from the story. Your product might be Captain Nips' Hot Potatoes or Hold-Your-Nose Billy's Garlic Ice Cream. Include one other character from *The Whipping Boy* in your commercial. Perform your commercial for the rest of the class.

- **Literary Interview**
  This report is done in pairs. One student pretends to be a character in the story. The other student will play the role of a television or radio interviewer, providing the audience with insights into the character's personality and life. It is the responsibility of the partners to create meaningful questions and appropriate responses.

- **What's in the Bag?**
  Decorate a paper sack with a picture of a scene or character from the book. Include the title, author, and illustrator. Place an item in the sack that relates to the story in some way. As you give an oral report of the book, pull out the mystery item as it fits in with your summary.

- **Design a Book Jacket**
  On white paper, make a book jacket for *The Whipping Boy*. Be sure to include the title, author, and yourself as illustrator on the front cover, along with the illustration. On the inside flap, write a summary of the book. On the back flap, write about the author.

Research Ideas

Describe three things you read about in *The Whipping Boy* that you want to learn more about.

1. _____

2. _____

3. _____

As you are reading *The Whipping Boy*, you will encounter interesting locations, people, and ways of life in a time period vastly different from your own. To increase your understanding of the characters and events in the story, as well as more fully recognize Sid Fleischman's craft as a writer, research to find out more about these people, places, and things.

Work in groups to investigate one of the areas you named above or the subjects that are mentioned below. Share your findings with the rest of the class in any appropriate form of oral presentation.

Medieval Europe

- Kings
- Lords
- Knights
- Princes
- Court jesters
- Bubonic plague
- Class system
- Heraldry
- Chivalry
- Clothing
- Jousting
- Whipping boys
- Dog-and-rat pits
- Castles

    -moats

    -drawbridges

    -crenels

Animals

- Ferrets
- Rats
- Bears
- Horses
- Peacocks
- Greyhounds
- Herring

Other

- Scientific research
- History of ballads
- Illiteracy
- Sewer systems
- Gypsies
- Newbery Medal books

Coat of Arms

In the Old World, those people of noble birth or great wealth had a family name shield or coat of arms. These shields contained symbols that showed the special or admirable traits of the family. Sometimes the shield contained the family surname (last name) or mottos such as **"Wisdom"** and **"Courage,"** or **"Strong Warrior."** It was customary for the coat of arms to be handed down from one generation to the next.

Have the students look over the list of symbols and meanings below. Instruct them to design their own family shields, choosing symbols that relate to their personality in some way. You might also suggest that the children create a motto and use their surnames on the shields. They may use the shield provided or make their own out of poster board.

heart	flower	tortoise	dragon
unicorn	lion	ship	swords
oldest son or daughter	2nd son	3rd son	4th son

Coat of Arms Pattern

If I Ruled the Kingdom

If you were a prince or princess about to inherit your parents' throne and reign as king or queen, what changes would you make when you become ruler? By what laws would you expect your subjects to live? Would you select a national anthem, motto, and flag to suit your individual tastes? Would you keep a whipping boy at the castle? How would you make your corner of the world a better place? Write about your ideal kingdom in the space provided.

An Award

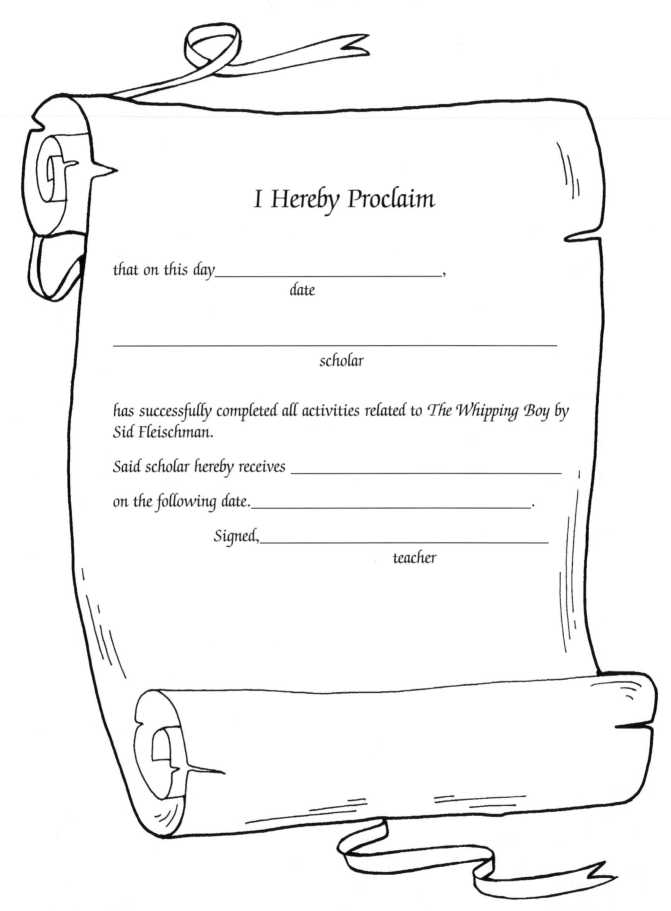

I Hereby Proclaim

that on this day_____,
                              date

_____
                              scholar

has successfully completed all activities related to *The Whipping Boy* by
Sid Fleischman.

Said scholar hereby receives _____

on the following date._____.

Signed,_____
                              teacher

Unit Test

Matching: Match the names of the characters with their descriptions.

_____ 1. Jemmy

_____ 2. Prince Brat

_____ 3. Master Peckwit

_____ 4. Hold-Your-Nose Billy

_____ 5. Cutwater

_____ 6. Betsy

_____ 7. Petunia

_____ 8. Captain Nips

_____ 9. Ol' Johnny Tosher

_____10. Smudge

      a. barefoot girl who owns a bear

      b. hairy outlaw who reeks of garlic

      c. a trained bear

      d. man who sells hot potatoes

      e. friend of Jemmy's

      f. spoiled boy who cannot read

      g. a whipping boy who loved to read

      h. a skinny outlaw

      i. a friend of Jemmy's father

      j. a frustrated teacher

True or False: Write true or false next to each statement below.

_____ 1. Jemmy had "lost his taste for ignorance."

_____ 2. Prince Brat's real name was Prince Morris.

_____ 3. Jemmy's father was a rat catcher.

_____ 4. The ransom note was written with beet juice and a hawk's feather.

_____ 5. Prince Brat is afraid of water.

Short Answer: Provide a short answer for each of these questions.

  1. Who are the villains in this novel? _____

  2. Ol' Johnny Tosher is disabled in what way?_____

  3. Discarded grain from the brewery attracts what animal? _____

  4. When does Prince Brat admit that he is afraid of the dark? _____

  5. Why does the king thank Jemmy?_____

Essay: Answer these questions on the back of this paper.

  1. Describe how friendship grows between Prince Brat and Jemmy.

  2. Explain what a *simile* is and write one of your own.

Response

Explain the meaning of each of these quotations from *The Whipping Boy*.

Chapter 1   *The young prince was known here and there (and just about everywhere else) as Prince Brat. Not even black cats would cross his path.*

Chapter 2   *'You fiddle-faddled scholar!' he bellowed. 'One day you'll be king! And you still don't know the alphabet from pig tracks!'*

Chapter 2   *'Take a last look at me, Pa, rest your bones,' he muttered to himself. 'Did you ever think I'd be holed up in the king's own castle and all rigged up in duds would shame a peacock? Reckon I'll fetch a pair of sharp-toothed ferrets and go to rat-catchin' same as you.'*

Chapter 3   *'But ain't you afraid of, the dark? Everyone knows that! You won't even sleep without a lit candle.'*

Chapter 4   *'Like a snake striking, a ghostly hand darted through the fog and clutched his arm.'*

Chapter 4   *'Slip away in the fog. Run for it! No more whippings for you, not if you can't be found. The great sewers, Jemmy, that's the place to hide!'*

Chapter 5   *'I am Prince Horace!' 'And I'm the Grand Turnip of China!' Cutwater snickered.*

Chapter 5   *'They ain't just common sparrows. Have a look at this saddle.'*

Chapter 6   *'Roll your eyes at this, Billy! Meat pies, looks like, and fruit tarts—and a brace of roast pheasant! We'll eat like kings!'*

Chapter 7   *'But how are we going to do the scribblement? We can't write.'*

Chapter 9   *The prince, he knew, had never been starved enough to pick out wildlife from his grub.*

Chapter 9   *'No, no, lad. Let's have it from bottom to top. Read it backwards.'*

Chapter 11 *'A horse can always find his way home, can't it?'*

Chapter 14 *'This is the first time no one has had fits because I got my clothes grimy.'*

Chapter 14 *'I might as well be stuffed and hung on the wall like a stag's head—for all he notices me.'*

Chapter 15 *'I've got to eat, don't I? If I can collect enough driftwood, I can sell it as firewood.'*

Chapter 15 *'Stop, Cap'n! We left me friend behind.'*

Chapter 16 *He'd dreamed of seeing the prince whipped, but now that it was happening he found no satisfaction in it.*

Chapter 18 *He saw no choice now but to return. But he realized that he'd lost his taste for ignorance.*

Chapter 19 *'I wish I were like you,' muttered the prince.*

Teacher Note: Choose an appropriate number of quotations for your students.

Conversations

Work in size-appropriate groups to write and perform the conversations that might have occurred in each of the following situations.

- At the king's grand feast, lords and ladies talk about the unruly prince and his behavior. *(4 or more people)*

- Master Peckwit talks to the king about the prince's schoolwork. *(2 people)*

- Billy and Cutwater discuss what they intend to do with the ransom money. *(2 people)*

- Jemmy tells Prince Brat of his life on the streets. *(2 people)*

- Prince Brat explains to Billy and Cutwater why he cannot read, even though he is the true prince. *(3 people)*

- Jemmy uses his best grammar to convince Billy and Cutwater that he is the true prince. *(3 people)*

- Billy and Cutwater explain to Jemmy and Prince Brat why they entered a life of crime. *(4 people)*

- Jemmy and Prince Brat argue about the prince's betraying him. *(2 people)*

- Upon receiving the ransom note, the king expresses concern over the safety of his precious son. *(2 or more people)*

- Jemmy meets the bear in the woods and tries to calmly talk the bear into leaving him alone. *(2 people)*

- Jemmy explains his situation to Betsy and asks for advice. *(2 people)*

- Prince Brat tells Jemmy and Betsy why he believes his father does not care about him. *(3 people)*

- Jemmy tells Betsy and Captain Nips how he felt when he saw the prince whipped. *(3 people)*

- Betsy scolds Billy and Cutwater for their meanness. *(3 people)*

- Jemmy, Prince Brat, Betsy, and Captain Nips discuss the fair at which Petunia will perform. *(4 people)*

- Smudge and Jemmy talk about old times. *(2 people)*

- Prince Brat confides in Jemmy about his fear of the dark. *(2 people)*

- Jemmy talks to the prince about his loneliness and missing his father. *(2 people)*

- Prince Brat apologizes to Jemmy for all the trouble he caused. *(2 people)*

- Jemmy and the prince discuss the importance of reading and writing. Betsy and Captain Nips agree with Jemmy. *(4 people)*

- Prince Brat and the king talk of ways to improve their relationship. *(2 people)*

- Write and perform one of your own conversation ideas for the characters from *The Whipping Boy*.

Bibliography of Related Reading

Fiction

Fleischman, Sid. *Chancy and the Grand Rascal.* (Little, Brown and Company, Inc., 1966)

Fleischman, Sid. *The Half-A-Moon Inn.* (Harper & Row, 1980)

Fleischman, Sid. *Humbug Mountain.* (Little, Brown and Company, 1978)

Fleischman, Sid. *Me and the Man on the Moon-eyed Horse.* (Little, Brown and Company, Inc., 1977)

Gwynn, Fred. *The King Who Rained.* (Windmill Books, Inc., 1970)

Kaye, M.M. *The Ordinary Princess.* (Doubleday & Co., Inc., 1980)

Noble, Trinka Hakes. *The King's Tea.* (Dial Press, 1979)

Scieszka, Jon. *The Frog Prince Continued.* (Viking, 1991)

Twain, Mark. *A Connecticut Yankee in King Arthur's Court.* (William Morrow & Co., 1988)

Twain, Mark. *The Prince and the Pauper.* (The World Publishing Co., 1948)

Nonfiction

Biesty, Stephen. *Cross-Sections Castles.* (Dorling Kindersley Publishing, Inc., 1994)

Cavendish, Marshall. *The End of Chivalry.* (Marshall Cavendish Corp, 1989)

Cavendish, Marshall. *The Middle Ages.* (Marshall Cavendish Corp., 1989)

Corbishley, Mike. *The Middle Ages.* (Facts on File, Inc., 1990)

Gravett, Christopher. *Castle.* (Alfred A. Knopf, Inc., 1994)

Gravett, Christopher. *Knight.* (Alfred A. Knopf, Inc., 1993)

Howarth, Sarah. *Medieval People.* (The Millbrook Press, 1992)

Morpurgo, Michael. *Arthur, High King of Britain.* (Harcourt Brace & Co., 1994)

Steele, Phillip. *Castles.* (Kingfisher, 1995)

Answer Key

Page 10

1. Accept appropriate responses.
2. Accept reasonable answers.
3. Answers may vary but should include tying powdered wigs of guests to the back of chairs, putting bullfrogs in the moat, and greasing the knights' saddles, causing them to slip off their horses.
4. As it was forbidden to spank a prince, the whipping boy is there to receive the prince's punishment for mischief.
5. Jemmy refuses to cry, yelp, or bellow during a whipping.
6. Master Peckwit is Prince Brat's tutor. He is frustrated and angry over the prince's refusal to learn.
7. Prince Brat does not see any value to learning to read and write, as he feels that he can always get someone else to write his name for him and read to him.
8. Jemmy hopes to "fetch a pair of sharp-toothed ferrets to go to rat-catchin'."
9. Prince Brat is afraid of the dark. He will not sleep without a lit candle.
10. The boys are grabbed by two highwaymen.

Page 15

1. Accept appropriate responses.
2. Billy is called "Hold-Your-Nose Billy" because he smells like garlic.
3. Cutwater first becomes aware that the boys are not ordinary when he notices the king's crest on the saddle of the prince's horse.
4. Jemmy has previously heard of the highwaymen in ballads sung in the streets.
5. Prince Brat's real name is Horace.
6. Jemmy thinks the prince was empty headed because he brings his crown as if he expects "vagabonds and cutthroats to fall to their knees."
7. Prince Brat brings meat pies, fruit tarts, roast pheasant, a china plate, silver spoon and knife, and a golden crown.
8. The outlaws believe Jemmy is the true prince because he can read and write and Prince Brat cannot.
9. Billy gives Jemmy a hawk's feather and beet juice to use as pen and ink.
10. For ransom, the bandits ask for a wagonload of gold and jewels.

Page 20

1. Accept appropriate responses.
2. He learns that those less fortunate often eat stale bread and food with worms in it.
3. Cutwater orders Jemmy to read the note backwards.
4. Jemmy intends to send the ransom note to the castle with Prince Brat, who the villains believe to be the whipping boy.
5. Jemmy intends to send the crown back to the palace to convince the king that the villains are genuine.
6. Accept appropriate answers.
7. The king knows his son could not have written the ransom note as he knows Prince Brat can neither read nor write.

Answer Key *(cont.)*

Page 20 (cont.)

8. Jemmy hides in the bedstraw.

9. Prince Brat thinks Jemmy intends to leave him alone with the villains.

10. The prince refuses to deliver the ransom note, so Jemmy suggests sending the king's horse. A horse can usually find his way home.

Page 25

1. Accept appropriate responses.

2. Jemmy meets a bear in the woods.

3. For a moment Jemmy is speechless. Then, he angrily tells the prince that he resigns as whipping boy.

4. Accept reasonable answers.

5. Betsy is looking for Petunia, her pet bear.

6. Mudlarking is collecting driftwood to sell as firewood.

7. Captain Harry Nips sells hot potatoes for a living. He gives the boys a ride in his coach.

8. Jemmy feels sorry for the prince, and he realizes how dependent upon him the prince has become.

9. Prince Brat does not betray Jemmy, probably because Jemmy had Captain Nips return for Prince Brat. One good turn deserves another.

10. Prince Brat does not holler or cry out. He only braces himself for the next blow.

Page 29

Explain to the students that their friendship journals can be evaluated in a number of ways. Here are a few ideas.

Entries will be read by the teacher, but no corrections or letter grades will be assigned. Credit is given for effort, and all students who sincerely try will be awarded credit. If a grade is desired for this type of entry, you could grade according to the number of journal entries for the number of journal assignments. For example, if five journal entries were assigned and the student conscientiously completes all five, then he or she should receive an "A."

Non-judgmental teacher responses should be made as you read the journals to let the students know that you are enjoying them. Here are some types of responses that will please the writers and encourage them to write more.

- "Your journal entries are thoughtful and well written."

- "WOW! This is interesting stuff."

- "You express yourself well, and your responses are very sincere."

- "You seem to be able to learn from this book and apply what you learn to your own life!"

- "I am proud of your effort!"

Page 30

1. Accept appropriate responses.

2. Jemmy feels no satisfaction in seeing the prince whipped, only a sense of amazement that the prince did not yell or bawl.

3. When Petunia pokes her head out the door window, the king's men wave the coach on.

4. The prince is hesitant to shake Smudge's hand because no one is allowed to shake hands with a prince.

Answer Key *(cont.)*

Page 30 (cont.)

5. The prince is deeply shaken to learn his subjects call him "Prince Brat."
6. According to the broadsides, the whipping boy is charged with selling the prince to the gypsies.
7. Ol' Johnny Tosher is a rat-catcher and had been a friend of Jemmy's pa.
8. The brewery workers empty used-up grain down in the sewers which attracts rats.
9. Betsy and Captain Nips receive the reward offered by the king for the return of Prince Horace.
10. Accept appropriate responses.

Page 42

Matching

1. g
2. f
3 j
4. b
5. h
6. a
7. c
8. d
9. i
10. e

True or False

1. True
2. False—Prince Brat's real name is Horace.
3. True
4. True
5. False—Prince Brat is afraid of the dark.

Short Answer

1. Hold-Your-Nose Billy & Cutwater
2. He is hard of hearing.
3. rats
4. in the sewers
5. for bringing the prince back home safe and sound

Essay

1. Accept appropriate responses. Answers should reflect all the boys have been through and how they began to see the good in one another in difficult circumstances.
2. Accept appropriate responses. Students should explain that a simile is a comparison of two objects using the words *like* or *as*.

Page 43

Accept all reasonable and well-supported answers.

Page 44

Perform the conversations in class. Ask students to respond to the conversations in several different ways, such as "Are the conversations realistic?" or "Are the words the characters say in keeping with their personalities?"